SUMMARY of

The Obesity Code

Unlocking the Secrets of Weight Loss

by Dr. Jason Fung and Timothy Noakes

A BriskReads Book Summary

Understand Main Takeaways & Analysis

TABLE OF CONTENTS

IN SUMMARY

For a long time, there have been several myths about losing weight. In the past, vanquishing obesity has implied hours of sweating on a treadmill and tallying grams of fat or calories. Fortunately, a valid key to losing weight is something a great deal more straightforward: hormones.

As this book will illustrate, insulin is an essential element for regulating metabolism, which controls weight gain. Put simply, insulin levels that are kept too high for a sustained amount of time leads to a resistance to insulin. That is the thing that makes individuals fat. Regardless of whether you are stressed over diabetes, or rushing to get to the nearest rec center to lose weight, the concepts in this book will instruct readers to understand how their diet is making things turn out badly.

LET'S GET STARTED

Any individual who has ever attempted to lose weight knows the enticement of imagining that the newest diet pattern of taking in fewer calories or keeping away from all fat will be the ideal approach to suddenly look incredible. Honestly, most individuals trust that you should only eliminate food intake and increase the quantity of pushups you do, or miles you run. However, for anybody attempting these reliable methods may ask themselves: if losing weight has nothing to do with what number of grams of fat or calories I put in my body, then is it truly just insulin?

Luckily, this book will clarify why those old methods aren't the answer to losing weight, using research to back it up. With regards to diabetes and losing a few (or many) pounds, most individuals are confused. Instead of taking a gander at what causes weight gain and diabetes, we focus on the symptoms. This means we spend hours doing laps and riding a stationary bike, just to discover we didn't shed one pound. Or, then again using crazy diets (grapefruit for seven days, anybody?) to see that nothing works. Far more detestable, we see individuals around us getting fit and trim. However, we do the same thing without any results. Or, on the other hand, we lose weight from dieting, however, gain each pound back, plus a few extra, the second we offer into our body's need for food.

Sadly, with such an overwhelming task, most individuals surrender. However, the uplifting news is that the answer to these mysteries is our hormones. This book will clarify how intermittent fasting can help you increase fixation, boost your energy, lastly get back into shape.

Important Points

- Losing weight successfully doesn't originate from crash diets or cutting calories and fat.

- Gaining weight in the wake of stopping a crash diet is normal, yet intermittent fasting is a long haul solution, permitting you to shed undesirable pounds

HOW DID OBESITY BECOME RAMPANT?

Because of the confusion of misinformation about obesity, many individuals have no clue what to accept. Most of the time, you go to a regular checkup for guidance about losing weight – just to see the specialist advising you to exercise all the more frequently and cut calories or fat from your diet is much more overweight than you are. Instead of taking after the balancing wisdom of fat doctors and old theories that don't work, it's time to find out about the causes of obesity.

Misunderstanding obesity has made the issue rampant. Much of the time, while dealing with a disease such as obesity, we tend to look at the adjoining causes instead of the real reason.

A nearby cause of obesity would take in significantly a bigger number of calories than you should, yet that is not the actual cause. Other adjoining causes would be not exercising enough or being too sluggish. There are even cases where individuals

Will be critical of your lifestyle choices, asserting you should deal with yourself better. However, looking at all of these adjoining causes won't solve the issue, because addressing the neighboring causes don't concentrate on the business at hand, which is the real cause of obesity.

Important Points

- As we consumed more processed foods, refined sugar and stopped eating natural fats and sugars, obesity turned into a widespread issue.

- The American Heart Association released a statement advising individuals to increase starch intake while decreasing fat intake. Instead of helping, the report prompted drastically increased rates of obesity.

OBESITY CAN BE INHERITED

Some families take after the regular pattern of obese parents prompting overweight youngsters. In spite of the fact that the modern believed is that factors in our environment caused this inherited characteristic. Be that as it may, when identical twins were adopted by various families yet still wound up being similarly obese to their biological parents, the environmental theory faltered. Mostly, this demonstrated the reason obesity is so prevalent is that it is inherited. So, if inherited genetics are causing obesity, why do experts keep on insisting that the intake of too many calories is the essential driver?

In the 1970s, a popular theory arose known as the thrifty-quality hypothesis. Finally, an association was made amongst genetics and obesity. In spite of the fact that food shortages stopped obesity, having an overabundance of food still did not ensure someone would be obese. Another defect in like manner critical theories on obesity incorporate the failure to distinguish between being obese and just being "fat." In the animal kingdom, a substantial bear purposely fattens himself before starting his long winter hibernation, because his body is intended to store a lot of food (counting fat) to use over a since quite a while ago, extended timeframe. This is the reason a bear doesn't confront severe wellbeing consequences for such seemingly dangerous conduct. Be that as it may, humans are not made for such over-consumption and directed long haul usage of food and fat.

Important Points

- Being obese is a hereditarily inherited condition. Absolutely, conduct and environment factors add to the issue. Be that as it may, these factors are not at the center of obesity.

- In spite of the fact that the animal kingdom can be sound while obese, humans have developed to support a slender body.

THE ERROR OF REDUCING CALORIES

A standout amongst the most dangerous assumptions made about obesity is that it is a result of taking in calories. First, people assume that calories and energy are the same as thermodynamic equations because what comes in must go out – in equivalent amounts. This means whatever you take in (calories) must be signed off in equal amounts, or the excess calories will be stored as fat. Be that as it may, this is yet another myth about obesity. Hormones control each system in the body, including flow, thyroid, and muscular. Body fat is regulated in the same path as these other body systems, by hormones. The worrisome truth is that many disregard the way that hormones direct fat intake, storage, and dissipation.

Another dangerous assumption is the possibility that each calorie is destructive. The simple truth is: that is not the situation. For instance, the calories found in olive oil are advantageous, as opposed to calories in refined sugar, which are to a great extent destructive. Working under the myth that calories are harmful, many people have drastically diminished their calorie intake to attempt and significantly lessen their fat (and obesity). However, studies have demonstrated that diminishment of calories doesn't ensure the decrease in weight. Honestly, it has been shown that there is no connection amongst calories and being overweight or obese.

Important Points

- Obesity is controlled by hormones, so emotional lessening in your intake of calories won't solve weight issues.

-

- Not all calories are made equivalent! Some calories are high, while others are horrendous – and each kind of calorie affects our body in unique ways.

EXERCISING: THE BIGGEST MYTH

In the mid-twentieth century, Americans started to focus on the need to increase (or start) an administration of physical activities and exercise. People trusted that the newest worries of obesity and coronary illness could be remedied by setting up exercise routines, created by a few gymnast experts. Bouncing on the temporary fad, the legislature spent a lot of cash persuading people to get up and get out there (running). However, in spite of the fact that the physical movement rates increased significantly, there was essentially no impact whatsoever on the rates of obesity.

Obviously, the way that increased physical action had no impact on obesity rates doesn't imply that it's unsafe to exercise. In any case, it does indicate that thinking exercise or physical movement will "consume off pounds" could be a blissful numbness. The human body is an incredibly proficient machine, ready to use its over-generation of calories for energy consumption and creation. So, considering the possibility of physical movement as a supernatural solution for obesity is just another myth.

Important Points

- Basic metabolic rates don't stay stable, and they are not constant. Like this, the decrease of calorie intake means the body will adjust itself – and use less energy, in the extent to the absence of calories.

- In spite of the fact that it's critical to exercise as a component of a fixed living schedule, it is not some enchantment solution that will settle obesity all alone.

THE PROBLEM WITH OVEREATING

A personal trainer named Sam Feltham did an experiment (on himself) on what might happen on the off chance that he substituted between a diet low in carbohydrates and a diet high in carbohydrates. The day by day intake of calories amid his experiment was just under 6,000 calories. As a result of this experiment, Feltham saw that in spite of the fact that he gained weight in both diets, the sort of weight he gained was altogether different. In the low-carb diet, he gained muscle mass; on the high-carb diet, he gained just fat.

At that point, in the 1960s, another man named Dr. Ethan Sims directed experiments (this time, on others) on obesity. First, he used lab mice; then, he switched to students and inmates at prisons. At the conclusion of his experiments, Dr. Sims found that it was to a significant degree hard to purposely make people obese. In the start of the experiments, some participants gained weight. Be that as it may, inside a short timeframe, the metabolic rate increased (to compensate), and their weight stabilized. Posttest body weight rates for participants tended to come back to typical. What the conclusion reached to by Sims was that gorging wasn't responsible for gaining weight forever, and not eating especially food didn't help participants lose weight for long.

At that point, Sims experimented with two different groups of extremely lean and exceptionally obese people. All the lean people were deliberately sustained too much. These fit people later gained weight, yet their metabolic rates increased, freeing their bodies of most of the new weight. However, the obese people's metabolism was slowed and almost stopped. The conclusion Dr. Sims came to is that the intake of more calories means your body will also consume more calories, which will give you more energy and help you dispose of the weight considerably faster.

Important Points

- To start with, overeating can make you gain pounds, however, if you stop then your body will rapidly re-stabilize, and your metabolic rate will increase.

- In spite of the fact that calories are a piece of the issue, regardless of whether you lose weight tends to depend more on metabolism rates.

HOPE, ALL OVER AGAIN

As things sometimes happen, when people discovered decreasing calorie intake didn't help free them of unwanted pounds, doctors took a page out of the oldest book: they reprimanded their patients for "not taking after the rules." Despite the way that experts knew increased food intake wasn't the primary cause of obesity, they kept on asserting that decreasing how much food people consumed would prompt the "destruction" of obesity. In the meantime, these experts deliberately overlooked the way that the body is almost altogether controlled by hormones. Truth be told, science has demonstrated that the way the human body works is about identical to something most of us can understand: a thermostat.

At the point when a thermostat tries to keep up a managed temperature, it must either be on warmth or cool. In any case, what might happen if both the warmer and AC were turned on simultaneously, in actuality engaging each other? The answer is that the thermostat would battle itself for the length of possible until it, at last, gave in – and broke. Our bodies are about identical. We start life with a genetic code that tells us what our ideal weight is (touched base at, by considering numerous factors, including genetics), just as a thermostat has its ideal temperature set. However, anytime we battle against our bodies to modify that ideal weight setting, we just have a temporary, minuscule amount of success. So, at whatever point someone stops dieting, they gain all the weight back they effectively lost – plus, a few extra pounds! So, who or what sets the ideal body weight for each of us? What's more, if our body's ideal weight is set too high, what would we be able to do? The answer is in hormones.

Fortunately, the theory of hormones being accountable for obesity, weight, and the decrease of weight is not just another false assumption or myth. The hormonal direction of weight explains that calories coming in and going out are entirely independent of each other and that hormones control the control of body weight.

Important Points

A protein named leptin was discovered, which drove scientists to yet another mistaken conviction that they had suddenly seen every one of the "answers" to losing weight. In any case, following several years of testing, scientists at long last needed to concede that leptin had absolutely nothing to do with decreasing obesity.

Albeit obese people are not "leptin-deficient," a large number of them show resistance to leptin.

INSULIN, ANYONE?

Prior, we discussed how the human body compares to a thermostat. Since it is a viable similarity, we should come back to that thought. Obviously, it's vital to diminish the ideal weight our bodies set, to ensure that our particular bodies don't "battle back" when we endeavor to either gain or lose weight. How can someone accomplish the seemingly impossible task of decreasing the ideal weight set by their particular bodies? All things considered, the answer is in understanding an essential hormone in the human body: insulin.

In studies where participants were infused with high doses of insulin, almost every one of them gained weight – at a huge rate. By the different token, those who have decreased their insulin have lost weight! Indeed, these people were found to have an over 20% plenitude of insulin, when contrasted with those who were less fatty.

Despite the fact that it is still obscure as to why and how an increase of insulin causes people to gain weight, it is still essential to realize that insulin is a vital part in the control of weight. Since we know insulin is a hormone – and that hormones control each system in our body – it's safe to say that insulin is either the cause or the cure for obesity, and obesity is an only hormonal issue.

Important Points

- Those who have diabetes commonly have low amounts of insulin in their bodies, which is the reason they experience such a fast loss of weight.

- Scientific studies have shown that weight loss caused by increased insulin levels is longer lasting than either exercising, dieting, or both!

THE CORTISOL HORMONE

Since we know the absence of insulin can cause dramatic weight increase, it's important to address another hormone: cortisol. This hormone, known as the stress hormone, is an important figure pushing us to activity. At the point when cortisol increases, more glucose is accessible for use, which then creates an incredible amount of energy for moving and running. In a dangerous situation, cortisol is the thing that guarantees the greater part of your available energy will be used to either stay and battle, or flee as fast as you can. This increase in cortisol is short-lived, which causes no medical problems. In any case, if cortisol becomes increased for a more drawn out term, problems arise.

Surely, the world is as of now a stressful place – both at home and at work. Many people confront serious subject matters, which as often as possible doesn't require any physical energy to be used. Be that as it may, with candidly stressful situations, cortisol is still made – however since it isn't used, the increased glucose levels transform into more insulin. Also, since an increase of insulin leads to a gain in weight, the answer is to decrease the cortisol so that insulin won't be increased. Truth be told, many results from experiments have shown that weight levels dropped as soon as the participants' stress/cortisol levels decreased. For instance, people who have Addison's disease encounter anomalous low levels of cortisol on a regular basis, which is the reason they lose weight quickly and rapidly.

Important Points

- Being denied of sleep means you have more cortisol in your system. So, if you get less than 7 to 8 hours of sleep at night, regardless of the possibility that you lessen your food intake, you will still gain more weight.

- In spite of the fact that not having enough sleep can make you obese, it is just a single of several factors (counting stress increases), which make you more obese.

NO, NOT THE ATKINS DIET!

Back in 1963, a man named Dr. Robert Atkins chose to attempt a diet low in carbohydrates. His results were irrefutably unimaginable! After such remarkable results, Dr. Atkins decided to share his diet with his patients, and informally made it a huge hit!

In any case, the American Heart Association refused to support Atkins' diet arrange, stubbornly standing by their particular decreased fat recommendations. Numerous physicians guaranteed that the risk of heart disappointment would increase, for followers of the Atkins diet. Be that as it may, since the AHA didn't show any confirmation for their claims, the Atkins diet fever proceeded. Many people lost weight on a diet, however, a greater part of followers stopped the diet after just a single year.

The most significant downsides of the Atkins diet were the restrictions against some of the most popular and "consoling" foods in the typical American diet: pasta, chocolate, refined sugar, most fruits, and white bread, among others. Because of such restrictive eating rules, many people who attempted to take after the diet at last fizzled – and all the emotional weight lost before all else were quickly gained back, plus some. Moreover, some the sugar restrictive reasoning behind the diet wasn't appearing well and good: Asian cultures, where rice is day by day staple of their diet, were observed to be even less inclined to weight gain than the regular Atkins-diet devotee.

Important Points

- First and foremost, followers of the Atkins diet may lose weight drastically; in any case, inside a few weeks or months, you will probably gain all the weight back (and that's just the beginning!)

- Understanding what causes obesity is crucial, because if calories, fat, and carbohydrates don't cause it – what in the hell is going on?

A HUGE PROBLEM:

RESISTANCE TO INSULIN

It takes the time to wind up plainly obese; slowly increasing our weight (pound by a pound) does not occur incidentally. Most diets are accelerated, with the expectation that the devotee should shed the weight rapidly. Further, although an increase in insulin levels causes people to gain weight, the resistance to insulin must not be overlooked.

How does insulin resistance function? The truth is that it's fundamentally the same as how someone becomes resistant to the euphoric effects of cocaine. A cocaine user who repeatedly uses the medication eventually becomes resistant to the vibe significant effects, so more is required for the same results. In the same route, exposure to high levels of insulin leads to greater weight gain. Sustained high levels of insulin aren't the main thing causing resistance. Hormones are usually created in spurts, in response to certain stimuli. Be that as it may, a constant amount of stimulus added to continuingly high levels of insulin creates the perfect storm of problems.

Just as having greater than normal levels of insulin can cause obesity, the threat increases when insulin is no longer effective. Being stuck in the cycle of obesity, stress, and the inability to adjust the levels of hormones leads to an extremely unhealthy and dangerous situation. Essentially, backpedaling to the thermostat comparison, a body that is resistant to insulin is a thermostat stuck too high/low.

Important Points

- Although people used to consume everything that was known to increase insulin (pasta, chocolate, refined sugar, white bread) most still didn't end up noticeably obese. Sustaining continuous high amounts of insulin is what leads to getting to be noticeably resistant.

- Currently, a nutritionist will advise you that eating at least six small meals for every day including snacks is ideal. Be that as it may, this guidance would prompt the destruction of the harmony between the states of being insulin deficient and insulin dominant.

TOO MUCH FOOD AND DIABETES SCIENCE

The American Heart Association built up the system of setting "Heart-check" symbols on any foods that were questionably unhealthy. Be that as it may, when this happened, there were countless amounts of snack items flooding the American market. Completely overlooking the issue of artificial sweeteners in a substantial portion of the meals, most people pointed the finger at calories for obesity.

Another misleading incident was an enormous myth caused by the marketing and food industries attempting to persuade the American open that calories found in garbage foods or sodas were the same as calories in healthy foods such as steamed asparagus. The food industry simultaneously told people in general that they should eat more food, all the more often! The truth is that snacking and eating all the more frequently makes it almost impossible to end up noticeably thin, not easier. Trying to consume colossal amounts of calories in one day by day dinner, then decreasing calories in the next supper to compensate has not been shown to work.

Additionally, numerous experts have prescribed that people have a huge dinner for breakfast each day, guaranteeing that not eating in the morning leads to increased craving throughout the day. In any case, the French culture substantially avoids breakfast (as an actual supper), leaning toward a measure of cappuccino or espresso with a croissant. Furthermore, the French are, in general, quite slim.

The truth about breakfast is that it can be just as small as a snack or light lunch because the hormones boosting our body don't require a lot of food to create more energy in the morning. All that is necessary is a small feast at the start of the day, to get your body up and moving!

Important Points

- Many people skip breakfast because of an absence of yearning or time, yet basic dieting myths continue to make people think they must eat a substantial supper, first thing in the morning.

- Don't eat, in case you're not ravenous, regardless of what people tell you.

OBESITY AND BEING POOR

In America, statistics demonstrate that obesity is on the rise. In states like Texas and Mississippi, the obesity rates are significantly higher than in others. Although it seems obvious that rich people would be more obese because of access to more food, the truth is that those in poverty are significantly more obese.

Although exercise is universally accessible – you don't need an expensive rec center membership to do pushups and run a mile – the reason needy people are more obese than the rich comes down to an availability of healthy foods. Any individual who buys steaks, cheeses, fresh fruits and vegetables from the market can attest to how expensive these foods are. Fast food restaurants are always advertising tremendous amounts of food at astonishingly low costs (double patty cheeseburger for just a dollar?)

Another issue causing poor people to be more obese is the government involvement. Welfare programs permit healthy choices, but some benefits are given to participants usually won't allow them to purchase such items. Also, the government subsidizes certain foods more than others – such as corn, used in the creation of high fructose corn syrup and other similar items high in sugar.

Important Points

- In the 1920s, sugar was extremely expensive, so just the rich could bear the cost of it. Not surprisingly, back then – the rich were all obese, while the poor were always too thin.

- Although many people accuse the advancement of technology and lifestyle (i.e. cars, computers) for their obesity, the center cause is still insulin.

FRUCTOSE IS DEADLY

Back in the 1970s, some Chinese citizens with diabetes were just 1%. Today – the rate of diabetes in China has surpassed Americans. In the past, Chinese people consumed rice as their staple food, so carbohydrate consumption wasn't the issue. The answer to the where the problem originated from was found in sodas. After the American open was no longer interested in soda advertising, companies shifted to the Asian market to increase profits.

Found in many fruits and natural products, fructose is ordinarily consumed. Be that as it may, eating fresh fruits just results in a fructose gain of around 20 grams for every day. Changing the fructose into corn syrup – which is sweet-tasting, addictive, and inexpensive to add to about everything – causes many adverse effects.

Fructose is considerably sweeter than glucose (which is better for humans), and it mixes better with most other processed foods. As with various seemingly gainful additives, the effects of this overprocessed sweetener were not studied until it was terribly late.

Important Points

- Although fructose seems great because it's natural, the liver is consistently stressed from the pressure of processing it in the body.

- The consumption of high fructose corn syrup leads to a fatty liver, which like this causes increased rates of those who are resistant to insulin.

DIET SODAS ARE NOT YOUR FRIEND

Thanks to the evils of refined sugar – increased heart problems and greater rates of obesity – the market was overwhelmed with each artificial sweetener scientists could create. Although studies showed aspartame causing malignancy in lab animals, it was still endorsed by the FDA. Then, sucralose supplanted aspartame, but it was also dangerous, and it's currently found in many diet sodas, gums, and candies. Sadly, people started to assume that since items didn't have the "underhanded sugar" in it (and therefore, fewer calories), those things were safe to eat or drink.

For a time, natural sweeteners such as agave nectar and Stevia wound up plainly accessible, but agave nectar was discarded when it was found to contain 80% fructose. Suddenly, experts were suggesting that diabetic patients use artificial sweeteners set up of "genuine sugar" because it was safe. The confirmation to back up these recommendations was either non-existent or not conclusive.

Researchers at long last took on the issue of artificial sweeteners, and the results were astonishing: not just dieted drinks not help people lose weight, it was causing them to get much more obese! Further, artificial sweeteners were found to cause heart-related health risks because they increased levels of insulin, and obesity was getting much more terrible.

Important Points

- Artificial sweeteners increase the cravings for sugar and food, as well as increase weight gain.

- Besides causing problems with weight gain and obesity, every artificial sweetener causes other health risks and issues.

FIBER THAT PROTECTS, AND HOW IT RELATES TO CARBS

After the Atkins diet "revolution," reduced carbohydrates seemed to be the thing everybody reprimanded for obesity. Despite the fact that many carbs make insulin levels spike, which then causes obesity, not all carbohydrates are awful. Another illustration is wheat. For a long time, wheat has been a standout amongst the most widely recognized staple foods in America. Now it is considered to be the cause of celiac disease because it contains gluten.

Another issue happens when people eat foods in a highly-concentrated shape. Eating too much at one time is never something to be thankful for. For instance, if you have twelve apples, you should not eat them at the same time. In any case, the standard American will consume a half-gallon of squeezed apple in one swallow, which is the same as having twelve apples. The same thing happens with wheat. Because of the way that wheat is processed now, it is stripped of every single healthy component, and the remaining wheat flour is absorbed into our bodies. Wheat (in its natural shape) has protective fiber that shields us from getting diabetes or obese.

Important Points

- Fiber is one of the best tools for fighting obesity because it leads to the reduction of food intake lowers insulin levels.

- In any case, fiber is also less tasty, so it is over-processed in most American foods, prompting new spurts of gluten allergies and sensitivities.

WHAT'S THE DEAL WITH PROTEIN?

An unevenness of carbs, fats, and proteins can prompt many issues in the body. Although we cannot create them ourselves, we must have things such as amino acids, and nutrients like omega-6 and omega-3. We also don't need sugars and carbohydrates as they are (especially processed) are completely unnecessary to our survival. Truly, carbs are quite nutritious for our diets, and although low-carb diets (like the Atkins diet) seem strange and ineffective, they are still quite healthy.

After it underwent a transformative process, the Atkins diet now prescribed high-protein, low-carb and low-fat foods. When experts understood that high-protein diets (similar to

refined carbs) could raise insulin terribly high, the dieting
industry was by and by developed.

Important Points

- On the off chance that glucose is given through IV or orally,
  glucose levels are identical. Insulin levels spike when
  glucose is taken orally.

- Although foods high in protein have fewer calories, they still
  cause insulin levels to increase.

FEAR OF FATS

Amid World War II, Dr. Ancel Keys noticed that despite the fact that Americans got better nutrition than European people, they were suffering from the risk of heart disease all the more often. As per Dr. Keys, the culprit was high levels of cholesterol. This claim was later observed to be another myth because ceasing consumption of cholesterol caused the liver to manufacture more.

Classifying foods leads nutritionists to three categories of fluctuated macronutrient: proteins,

Carbohydrates, and Fats. There are much more divisions of fats: trans, saturated, and unsaturated. The carbohydrates are separated into unpredictable and straightforward. Although this made things easier to understand, it didn't assist with the hundreds of phytochemicals and nutrients that were necessary to keep metabolic rates regulated.

Important Points

- Because of its fat grams, avocados used to be considered "awful" for you. In any case, now it is regarded as a superfood, because of the various nutritional benefits.

- Although the dangers of butter and animal fats have been broadly promoted, artificial foods such as margarine are a great deal more dangerous.

WHAT CAN YOU EAT?

At whatever point you take after faddish diets like Mediterranean, Atkins, or low-calorie versions, you will lose weight at the outset. Be that as it may, you will eventually hit a plateau and regain the greater part of the weight you lost, because of increasing insulin levels. This is the reason it is so important to consider both the short-term and long haul effects of weight loss plans while choosing the diet you might take after.

Obesity is not caused by any one factor. In fact, there are multiple, perplexing factors that consolidate to cause obesity, including carbohydrates, fat, high fructose corn syrup, calories, and increased insulin (or insulin resistance). Focusing on just a single cause of obesity won't be an effective solution. Just as heart disease that comes from a long line of family genetics, age, lifestyle choices, sexual orientation, and other factors – obesity is also caused by a wide range of joined factors.

Important Points

- The best solution for an effective diet is to focus on bringing down carbs, calories, and fat – or any combination, thereof.

- Treating obesity just works when you, at last, discover why you wound up noticeably obese, in the first place. For instance, on the off chance that you are consistently inadequate with regards to sleep, it's important to correct your sleep patterns before you stress over sugar intake.

SO, WHEN SHOULD I EAT?

Although focusing on what you eat (your diet) is important in the management of obesity, it's not the main thing. Another important focus point is the point at which you eat. Anytime your body is consistently managing high levels of insulin; there is a constant, progressing battle with losing weight. The downside is that, regardless of the possibility that you eat less, the battle will eventually be lost because supper timing could be the issue.

There are some foods that prevent high levels of insulin, but they don't bring down levels of insulin. This means that the best approach to lessen insulin is a traditionally used cure known as fasting. When you occasionally fast (known as intermittent fasting), you can go somewhere in the range of one day to 36 hours without eating. Despite numerous physicians saying the practice is not good for you, there are significant health benefits, which cannot be overlooked.

Important Points

Not eating for short amounts of time is called intermittent fasting. When you take after this type of fasting administration, it will bring down insulin levels, which increases the body's ability to lose weight.

Starvation is not the same thing as fasting. Starvation is something that you don't readily do; it's something that happens because you have no ability to control it. Fasting is voluntary (you choose to do it), as well as both controlled and very much arranged.

Thank You

For Reading

62038911R00038

Made in the USA
Middletown, DE
18 January 2018